WODEN DOG

Woden Dog was first printed in *PN Review*.

This project is in part supported by a grant from the National Endowment for the Arts in Washington, D.C., a federal agency.

Burning Deck is an affiliate of Anyart (5 Steeple St., Providence, RI), a non-profit organization.

CHRISTOPHER MIDDLETON

Woden Dog

BURNING DECK
Providence

Wot doth woden dog
Por dog drageth plow

Thing odd dog not
Much good plow drager

But por dog drageth
All same plow

More come jellifish
Sting him woden dog

Jellifish in air now
Other odd thing

A speeking maner come
Round back to trooth

So doth dog plow
Plant seed of tree

Por dog life short
Woden dog long hope

Woden dog keep stung
Jellifish all round back

Dog hope tree grow
Much tree grow soon

Dog want find tree
Find releaf releaf

Bus drifer pleez
Make a smoth start
If not woden dog fall over

Bus drifer stop graduel
If not woden
Dog hit deck

Pleez bus drifer
Tern corner sofly
Woden dog cant hold on.

You no he cant sit
Propper
You no he cant holtite

Forgoet how to life has he
Lest thing nock him sensles
All you no

Woden dog smoth graduel
Woden dog sofly he scare think
You forgoet how to drife

Jakit off jus warin sox like mean you
Woden dog reed times ever doggone day
Nites watchin his toob wow
Haffin the noose hapn

Wow fokes I tel you
Woden dog lap up noose
Woden dog bominate seecrit he reely do
Noose noose he bark runnin down street
Galumfin baknforth to his malebocks

He wannit so bad
He wannit to go
Like choclit maltn ketchup
Hole globe pakitchn pree paredn paid fur
Sitn in his noose baskit

No seecrit make woden dog
Bust out in flour one mawnin
Lookit soaps he buy woden dogfood
Killins toon that po looshn stuf
Brung home in his teeth

Come days wen he skratchn say
Mite try killin sumwun to make noose of me
Paps if I make noose off him
He dont done do it?

Woden dog howcom you loss
Yor own seecrit eye sunshine
Woden dog howsit taist that woden dogfood
Whars thet kemel dog
Ever see canser wok a mile
Smokin up a kemel ever see war stop
Juscos you lookin?

Jeez fokes jus thort
If bad stuf stop no mor noose fur woden dog
Wot then ole flee bit dog
You see nuddin to lookat
You jus sit theren cry

Whodat
Striden backnforth in orifice
Who dat
Givin ordures

Whodat maken long biznis calls
Eatin long biznis bananas
He look horty
My whodat planifikting plitical fouture

Watchout
Here he come zoom by
Zoom silva jet clatter copta
Weekend in Toekyoe?
Meetin Younited Nayshun?

Whodat now
Widda dame in a yot wearin captin hat
Crakin lobsta
My my

Woden dog thats who
Woden dog how smart you done got

Hard inside
Woden dog

Woden dog gon
Sniff aroun for mudder

Mudder soft inside
Woden dog dig

Woden dog swetpant
Nuddin come up

No mudder
Dipressed woden dog

Dog shrink gifm pill
How that now help

Dog body keep movin
But inside he nut

No mudder inside
No soft strong mudder

Nuddin in world
Woden dog size

Howls too purty offen
In his dog house dum

So small he feel
Stinkin wikid woden

Yes derm dawg
Urmpteen snarls
Make nuddin
No bedder

Yew always countin
Countin crazy dawg
You mean
See me through glass

Derm yew lukn so glum
Like eny doods nuddin
Yew like like yew
Say dancein shit

Call yewsell a dawg
I aint buyin
Yew aint no morna
Cardbord ratlsnaik

Yew mean
Snarlin always makin
Fuss yew bossy think
Me mor stoopidn yew

Maybe too
But I countin
The timesnile git yew
Wunofem

Woden dog keep stil
So you can feel it
Movin

Rounanroun whirlin world
Why you keep with it
Is that reel

Woden dog
Keep stil so you
Can feel it movin

Hey now
Hoo done got hide
Inside you innerlekshuls

Meckin
Yore gin
Roll I say shuns

Hooz
Moovin yoohoo
All ways tokkin

Wokkin long
Rode like you wuz
Uh ginrollized creekin

Rekkernize hoo
He be my my if it aint are
Ole solom fren dubble you dee

Woden dog sittin
On the backstares

Sittin in the dark
Breathin a bit

What's this listen
Breathin

Laff
Woden dog

That's it
Laffin on the backstares

Thems wavesnwaves
Them cool backstares

Help dog floatin
Low float high

Not let waves go so
You seem zikazak

Doan it hurt some
Hey woden dog

Not let the laff hole up
In woden dog box

Listen breathin just so
Now no more done hurt

Wyso suddn everbody
Rite on walls

FREE WODEN DOG
Anifs time

Like I nevver got
Inclose free

Woden
Dog piksher?

Spose no place else
To rite

Silva smoak of pine
Burn chill
Woden dog shivver
Owl not heard

Lightslice fix to floor
Think dead
Woden dog like ice
In his box owl not heard

Owl hoot rainbow
Out of owl eyes
Owl hoot rainbow wonder
Dog not see dog bark at ghost

Owl not heard
Dog munch heap white aple
Not feel snow as owl bountie
Not smell snow rainbow

Woden dog eat heap
Aple up
Pip corn all cold aple meat
Not see owl

Not see some owl eyes
Not hear
How pips look sound yum yum
Crunch owl eyes aple up

Dog wine in boxn stay putn scoff
Woden dog alltime scoff
Woden dog shut in wod
Not smell sweet pine

Woden dog not smell wind song
Burn swingin low
Swingin in pine wod
Owl not hoot fur him in pine log

Owl not hear in dog box
He woden dog
Snow owl hoot that rainbow now
Now hootn touch dog heart

This booklet was designed & printed by Keith Waldrop. The text was linotyped in 12 pt. Palatino Italics by Mollohan Typesetting in West Warwick. There are 500 copies on Warren's Olde Style and 26 signed copies on Barcham Green Charter Oak, lettered A-Z.